HOW TO SELL
100 CARS A MONTH

by
Ali Reda and Damian Boudreaux

Printed in the United States of America
Print ISBN 978-1-944602-07-9
Ebook ISBN 978-1-944602-08-6

Thanet House Publishing
848 N. Rainbow Blvd. #750
Las Vegas, NV 89107

Cover Design by: Michael Hunter
Website: AutoTrainingAcademy.com

Ali's Dedication and Acknowledgements

To my Mom: I owe you everything for instilling great values in me and teaching me to be compassionate towards others.

To my wife, Lina, and kids, Michael and Madina, for the sacrifices you make on a daily basis. You are always there for me, and I'm truly blessed to have you all in my life.

To my brother Sam who is always by my side and my biggest supporter. Love you all.

Special thanks to my mentor, Jerry Turfe, who taught me just about everything I know. And Bobby Kapp who believed in me enough to give me my first auto sales job and helped guide me along the way. And Scott Montgomery for being a great friend and helping me get to the next level. I couldn't have done it without you. Thank you for all your love and support. Love you all.

Damian's Dedication and Acknowledgements

To every sales person looking for a different way to succeed beyond their wildest dreams. Whatever your dreams—you can reach them!

Thank you to my friends and mentors: Ali Reda, Bob Mohr, Scott Montgomery, Denise McIntyre, Michelle Smith, Jenni Robbins, Alec Savoie, Michael Hunter, Mike Good, David Saied, Thomas Carnivale, Greg Cole, John Kostakos, Mark Maness, Lynn Thomas, Mel Abraham, Brendon Burchard, Roger Love.

And special thanks to Tracey Charlebois and Julie Anne Eason. Without you, this book wouldn't exist.

Before We Get Started . . .

Take a minute and fill in these questions.
It will help.

Why do customers buy from you?

How many cars do you currently sell each month?

What's your dream? How many cars would you be happy selling?

Contents

Foreword

Most sales managers would describe the "perfect sales person" as someone who can sell 12-15 cars a month, not cause any drama, and have perfect CSI scores. That's the dream for us!

What if I could show you someone who has all those characteristics AND sells over 100 cars a month?

My name is Scott Montgomery, and I'm the General Sales Manager at Les Stanford Chevrolet Cadillac in Dearborn, Michigan. Ali Reda is one of my sales people.

A lot of people think Ali's story is incredible—as in, they don't really believe it. They think he must be some kind of prima donna, or a robot, or that he must have some sweet company fleet deals that boost his numbers. That couldn't be farther from the truth. He is a consummate gentleman, always ready to help others.

He's currently averaging 115 cars a month. He was at 122 last month. This year he's at 1250 units delivered, and it's only the middle of December. Obviously, he's talented. In addition to that, he's a consummate professional, constantly refining his skills and learning new ways to master his trade. That's what Ali does. He is off the charts at getting the work done and being a master sales person.

Ali wasn't born with some magic ability to sell cars. He doesn't even keep track of the numbers anymore. At the end of the month, I have to track him down and tell him how many cars he's sold. He's too focused on helping the next customer to worry about counting up yesterday's units.

He's selling 115 General Motors products a month in the home of Henry Ford. We actually share a property line with the Henry Ford Museum. It's not easy to sell GMs in this town! But at the end of the day, Ali is a relationship guy. He will do anything for his customers. They are like his family.

If it were 3:00 in the morning and I had to rush my wife to the hospital, I'd call Ali and say, "Hey, man, I'm dropping my kids off at your place."

He would say, "Don't bother dropping them off. I'm on my way over." That's the kind of dedication he has for everyone he works with. He's completely selfless. When there's snow on the ground and there are cars to move, he's the first one out the door. When it comes down to another sales person needing a certain car that he needs, he *always* gives up the car. Not just now and then. Always.

He's never part of "the huddle" when a bunch of sales people gather together to complain about something going on or talk about yesterday's baseball game. That's just not a productive use of his time, so he doesn't participate.

Ali is highly consistent. He has to be to keep everything straight. Everyone has to get the same deal every time. He won't let one of his customers get a car for $250 a month, and then sell someone else the same car for $190. He never waits on Ups. He leaves those for the other sales people. He is 100% in the relationship business.

He is smooth as a swan. And just like a swan, he looks smooth on the top, but under the water his feet are churning 100 miles an hour. Yet he only works five days a week, *never* sells fleet, and only has a couple of people helping him out—one to handle the paperwork and scheduling, and one to take care of the little logistical details on deliveries.

I can honestly say I used to think selling 100 cars a month was impossible. Not only have we learned it *is* possible, it's become a way of life. It's just the way things are. No big deal.

Now, I'm sure you're a great person, happy to help others, eager to get customers into the right cars—but maybe you feel lucky to sell 12 or 20 cars a month. Ali and Damian's training will help you get to the next level—whatever that is for you. If Ali can do it, so can you.

Pay attention to the lessons in this book. Learn them. DO them. And you will succeed at whatever level you want.

I wish you all the success in the world!

Scott Montgomery
GSM, Les Stanford Chevrolet Cadillac

Everything is Impossible
Until It's Done

Hi there. My name is Ali Reda, and I sell cars for a living. I sell a *lot* of cars—usually around 100 a month these days. My best month so far was 144.

Does that seem impossible to you?

I get that. It seemed impossible to me, too. Until I did it. Everything in life is impossible, until it's done. Then it's inevitable.

Think about it for a minute. How many things do we take for granted every day that were once considered impossible? Human beings can't fly—it's impossible. We can't walk on the moon—it's impossible. We can't communicate with people on the other side of the world—it's impossible. Yet today, we have airplanes and spaceships, telephones and the internet. All those formerly impossible things are now commonplace.

A little over 60 years ago, people thought no one could run a mile faster than 4 minutes and 1 second. It was just accepted that the human body could not push itself faster than that. The four-minute mile was the barrier. It was impossible to beat. Then a young man named Roger

Bannister woke up on the morning of May 6th, 1954, and broke that barrier. An amateur athlete who spent more time studying science than training ran the mile in 3:59:4.

And suddenly, it was possible.

It only took one person to prove it, then everyone knew the barrier had no meaning. Bannister held the world record for 46 days when John Landy ran the mile in 3:58. Over the next few decades, that record has inched down to 3:43. It's still a major feat of human determination to run a mile in less than 4 minutes, no doubt. But it is possible. And that's all we need to know to make it happen.

For Many Sales People, 100 Cars a Month is the 4-Minute Mile

It seems impossible. No one can sell 100 cars a month. Can they? Well, yes, they can. And you can, too. All you need are two things.

1. You need to believe it's possible.
2. You need to decide you want to do it.

Once you have those two pieces of the puzzle firmly in place, your brain will start seeking out ways to make it happen. You'll start thinking in new ways. You'll approach your job differently. And that's what has to happen.

You have to think about your job and the car business as a whole in a different way, if you want to reach those higher levels.

In this book, I'm going to show you how I do it. The idea is to inspire you. To show you that the barrier you think is there, really isn't. Just like the 4-minute mile, 100 cars a month is achievable.

Is it going to happen next month? Probably not, unless you're currently at the 60 - 75 level already. But that's okay. This isn't a get-rich-quick scheme. It's not a secret word track or crazy closing process. It's a mindset. It's a different way of doing business that sets you apart from everyone else who's selling the exact same thing in the exact same place. And this approach to the car business takes time to develop, grow, and bear fruit.

By the time you finish reading this book, you will understand what I'm talking about. And you will be so relieved that it's not difficult or awkward. In fact, it's the opposite of difficult and awkward. It's natural and hardly feels like selling at all.

Why Are We Writing This Book?

There are plenty of sales books out there, including books on how to sell cars. In fact, my friend, coach and co-author, Damian Boudreaux, has written two of them, *Keep it Simple Selling* and *Keep it Simple Success*. So, why write another one?

We want you to know what's possible. We want to open your eyes, raise your awareness, and completely shift your world. As Damian likes to say, the car business is a gold mine. But you have to approach it the right way.

This book is all about getting to the next level. Whatever that is for you at the moment. You might not get to 100. You might not even care to get to 100. Maybe 45 would rock your world. The number itself doesn't matter. What matters is continually raising your awareness of what's possible. And challenging yourself to get to that next milestone.

I can remember the first time I sat in one of Damian's sales seminars and listened to him talking about a few of his friends. One person stood out in my mind. Greg Cole. At that time, he was selling 50 Toyotas a month. And that was my 4-minute mile. If he could do it, so could I.

That's what I want for you. I want you to open your eyes and see that the only thing holding you back is your belief in what's possible.

Another reason we're writing this book is to change the image of the car salesman. Most people think sales people like us are somehow sleazy, dishonest, and out to take advantage of them. I hate that! It's not true for me. It's not true for Damian. And it doesn't have to be true for you, either. The beautiful thing about how we do business, and how we reach such high numbers, is that we *aren't* sleazy or dishonest. We treat people like royalty. We love helping people. And we're never pushy or obnoxious.

That's why the public likes doing business with us. That's why we can sell 100 or more—because our approach is different. You can't get to the higher levels in this business if you're dishonest. If you treat a customer badly just once, it's all over social media, and you have to start building your reputation all over again.

This Works for All Kinds of Sales

You don't sell cars? That's okay. It doesn't matter whether you sell trucks, boats, RVs, motorcycles, or houses. Heck, this even works if you're selling insurance or appliances. The process works best if your product is something people need to buy more than once. But the mindset is the same. So, even though I'm going to talk about cars throughout this book, feel free to substitute in whatever your particular product is.

You Might Be Thinking . . .

People often tell me they think it's nice that I can sell 100 cars, but they can't do it because _____. Then fill in the blank with their favorite objection. They don't have time. They live in the wrong place. Their manager is a jerk. Blah, blah, blah.

Let me tell you something about objections. They always seem rational. They make perfect sense. There's no way you can sell more than 20 cars because you're already working 7 days a week, right? But the truth is you can. You just have to be open to a different mindset, a shift in your way of thinking about the challenges.

You CAN sell 100 cars with one assistant, while working less. Really! I have one assistant and I only work 5 days a week. I know that seems crazy in the car business. Nobody takes the weekends off, right? Well, I do. And I bet you'd like to, if you could figure out a way. Am I right?

We're going to address all the "reasons" you might think you can't do this in a later chapter. For now, I want you to consider the idea that maybe all your reasons are just distracting you from the truth. Suspend your disbelief and put your objections away—just for a little while.

For now, believe it's possible. Others have done it. Therefore, you can do it, too.

And even if you don't believe it's possible for you to reach 100, find the number you *can* believe in. What's your next level? If you're currently selling between 7 and 15 cars a month, maybe your 4-minute mile is 25. If you sell 30 now, maybe 45 seems like a crazy goal. It's all about incremental improvement.

Get excited! You're going to have lots of Roger Bannister moments in your career as you bust through every barrier and set your sights on the next one.

Damian's Story
(In His Own Words)

I got into this business because I was two months behind on my rent and nobody else would hire me. My friend hired me to clean parts at his transmission shop at night, and I was so grateful. I would go to work every night cleaning transmission parts, and I loved it. He and I got to be good friends. After about 60 days, he decided it might be better if I sold cars. I have no idea where he came up with that idea, but he opened up a used car lot and put me in charge. It was called Broad Street Auto Sales, and it only took about 4 months for him to fire me. There was no way I was qualified to run a business, it's just not in my nature.

I needed to get another job. So I went down the street to the local Chevrolet store, and they hired me to change oil. Exactly 30 days later, the owner sold the dealership. The new owner knew my family and was happy to see me there, and for some crazy reason, he decided I should sell cars. He said he would pay me minimum wage for as many hours as I wanted to work. Now let me tell you, I can work some hours! I'm not afraid to work. I'll work 80 hours a week, if I can. They also gave me a little Cavalier to drive, so I didn't have to drive that old Mercury anymore. I had a brand new car! I was so excited to get to work, and I talked to everyone I knew. That first paycheck, I made $1,600. I was rich! I paid off my back rent. I bought my future ex-wife some flowers. And I got a manicure because I'd always wanted to have one.

I called my dad and told him I was going to be rich. I had never seen $1,600 in my whole life. And that started my journey selling automobiles.

Remember that myth about beginner's luck? I slammed into it like it was a brick wall. I watched people, and I learned. I became a serious student of the car sales business. As hard as I tried, and as many hours as I worked, I was stuck between 7 to 12 cars a month. Now you might think, that's not so bad. But it is bad when there are people at the dealership selling 20 to 25 cars every month. I compared myself to them and thought what do they have that I don't? Why are they better than me?

It wasn't always like that. There were some months where I was almost salesman of the month. Of course, the next month I was almost fired. Then the next, I was almost salesman of the month again. I went up and down and up and down. It was frustrating, and I was exhausted!

The worst part was, I knew I was better. I had this number in my head—26 cars. I'm supposed to sell 26. But you can't sell 26, if you can't break 20. So 20 became my Roger Bannister barrier. If I could only break

20, then I could get to 26. So, I busted my butt. I talked to everybody. I was running to greet people. Sure enough, on the 20th of the month, I had 16 cars. I thought, I got this. It's finally going to happen.

And as soon as I thought *I got it*, a great big invisible Sabotage Button appeared out of nowhere, and I pressed it. I blew my success to smithereens! F&I helped by kicking back three perfectly good deals for some crazy reason. My managers were yelling at me for something I didn't have anything to do with this time. My future ex-wife was yelling at me for forgetting to take the garbage out on Thursday. I don't even remember when Thursday is…and, anyway, you cooked the garbage, you take it out! And thank goodness I got a toothache. Where'd that come from? I'd never had a toothache before—that's crazy.

I ended up with 18 cars for the month. My business was up and down, survival to almost successful.

I was miserable. I was frustrated. I was angry. And I was done. That's it. I'M IN THE WRONG BUSINESS! There's no other explanation. It's supposed to be easier. In this dealership, there were 6 other people selling more than 26 cars a month. And they were no better than me. I just couldn't figure out what they were doing differently. Maybe they were getting all the house deals, and the managers were feeding them solid. But one guy sold 40 cars a month, and he wasn't any better than me. I quit!

Only my manager wouldn't let me quit. He believed in me and said I just needed to take some time off because I was too emotional. He said I should go back to Louisiana and go hunting or fishing or cooking or whatever it was we do back there. Then if I came back and still wanted to quit, he would let me quit.

So I did. I took a leave of absence, and I went home. I drove two and a half hours back to Lake Charles, and I saw the world I grew up in totally differently. For the first time, I saw my home and my family from the outside. I could look at it more objectively because I had been away. I went to my dad's drug store and really watched him for the first time. Now, my family had owned the drug store since 1923, and I had been working there since I was a kid. But for some reason, I saw something new this time.

I watched my dad and my Uncle Jerry as they loved and cared for patients. If you couldn't afford your medicine, your medicine was free. They were not there to sell cough syrup or a prescription. They were there to solve people's health needs. They were not attached to the money. They were attached to the customer's good health. They were mission driven. My eyes opened wide and I felt like I'd just seen the sun after living a year underground. I watched them treat people like royalty. They weren't selling anything; they were solving problems.

I learned a lot more from my father during my time back home. When I finally went back to Houston, I decided I was going to try selling the way he did. I was going to talk to people and be 100 percent present with them. I was going to ask questions until I got the picture about what they wanted or needed. And I was going to care more about the people than the money. And it didn't take long before I blew past my 26 car goal and started selling 30, 40, 60 cars a month. My best month was 102 cars.

Maybe you're like me. You want to be successful. You want the shiny car and the big house and the awesome bank account. You want your family to be secure, and you want the freedom of having your own business. You want to be proud of what you do. But you don't have those things. You don't have that feeling. You're struggling. And you just want to figure out how to make the process work.

This industry has meant so much to me and my family, and I want it to fit for you. For years, I've been teaching about what I learned from my father. I wrote a book about it. And I've helped people like Ali expand their horizons and reach goals they never dreamed possible.

I take care of people. It's what I've always done. And it's what I'll always do.

Here's My Story

The first time I heard Damian speak, I had only been at the dealership a couple of days. I had just come from another store where I was selling around 35 cars a month already. I knew I could get back to that range, even though I was starting over at a new location. He asked me what number I wanted to get to. Being bold, I said 60. I remember thinking *if I can get to 60, that would be amazing!* At the end of that seminar, I *believed* that I could do it. By the time I went home that evening, I knew people already doing those numbers.

If you tell someone doing 20 that they can do 100, it's not believable. That's too big of a stretch. But tell them they can do 45, and they'll try. They'll push themselves and reach new levels. Then once they're at 45, you can push them to 60. That's how I learned to think about my numbers. Just get to the next level. And the next. And the next.

The first time I hit 50, it was an unbelievable feeling. I could always get close, but *nobody* I knew was hitting 50. It was the barrier. Then when I finally crossed the barrier, I sold 51. I did it working 5 days a week, but I worked really long 16-hour days.

I remember calling Damian and sharing how happy I was. How successful I felt. I couldn't believe that it felt so effortless. He immediately asked, *what's the next number and how do you get there while working less?* I told him 70. And he helped me believe I could hit that goal as well. He showed me what I needed to do to reduce the stress levels and sell even more—get an assistant. Once I had the right help, I jumped from 50 to 70 really quickly. And then 101 was just around the corner.

Momentum is an amazing thing. I've stopped even thinking about the numbers, they just happen. There's no break in the action because I'm just serving people as fast as I can. And the sales just pile up. It's a constant stream of customers, no matter what time of the month. My best month was 144, and I didn't even know we'd hit that until days later.

Every time I hit a new milestone, I'd call Damian because he was as excited as I was. He served as my mentor and the one person I could count on to help me. It wasn't like a typical coaching arrangement where two people try to get past roadblocks and obstacles. For us, it was more about pinpointing what I was doing right and finding ways to do more of the right things. It was all about smoothing the way and clearing out the time-wasters and inefficiencies. He was always pushing me to the next level—the next number goal. Meeting and maintaining high volume sales is not about working harder. It's about working *smarter*. And a coach or mentor really helps with that because they can see what you can't.

Eventually we switched from focusing on more and more cars per month to how I could add to the revenue for each car sold. An extra $100 per person is nothing. But when you multiply that by 100 cars per month, it adds up quick. I never looked at the money as a motivator for reaching the next level. I just wanted to hit the next big number.

The numbers and *the people behind the numbers* were motivating. Even now, I don't think about it. I just know that high volume equals a lot of money. So, I focus on the volume. There's always something more I can do, more people I can serve. High achievers always want more, no matter how well they're doing. And there's nothing wrong with that. It's a challenge to be met.

A little while back, I was sitting in one of Damian's seminars when he asked the group if they knew anyone who had ever sold 100 cars in a month. The men and women in the audience looked around with blank stares on their faces. Some of them were looking at him like he was completely full of it.

He asked them if they'd like to learn from someone selling 100. Every hand shot up. Then he asked, *How many of you would like to meet someone who is doing 100*, and he had me stand up.

You could have heard a pin drop. I can still feel the energy from every single person in that room looking at me. I can still feel how the entire room shifted in that moment. One minute they had a 4-minute mile barrier. The next minute, they didn't. Once they saw me stand up and had a chance to talk to me, their worlds would never be the same again.

The smiles on their faces. The excited chatter. The electricity in the room. I want that for you, too. I'm not writing all this down to brag or make you feel less accomplished. I'm doing it to replicate the feeling in that room. So that *anyone* who wants to raise the bar on their own sales numbers will believe they can.

Are you starting to see the possibilities?

Damian's Model

Why You CAN'T Sell 100 Cars a Month . . .

(Yet)

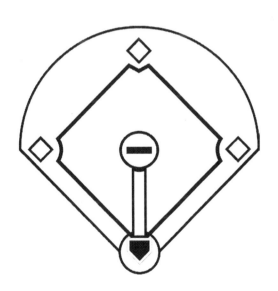

Take a look at the baseball diamond above. When you're playing baseball, the goal is to get on first base, right? You just want to get a hit. Traditionally, that's what our industry teaches you how to do. They teach you to swing at the pitches (the Ups) and hopefully sell a car (get to first base). They don't teach you to get to second base, or third. And if selling 100 cars a month is considered a home run—well, you can't do it with what they've taught you. Here's why:

The industry teaches a *transactional* model based on dealer-driven opportunities (or Ups). You know the drill, right? You go out on the floor, talk to people who come in the door, call, or inquire over the Internet, and some of them buy a vehicle. If you follow your training, you'll manage to sell somewhere around 20% of the people you talk to. That means if you swing the bat 60 times, you're going to sell somewhere between 10 and 14 a month. The only way to increase that number is to wait on more dealer-driven opportunities or increase your closing ratio.

To get to 100 vehicles a month at a 20% closing ratio means you have to wait on 500 people. That's 25 people per day working 5 days a week so that you can spend time with your family a couple of days aweek. You might want to go fishing, attend a ball game, or just get home early enough to watch Wheel-of-Fortune at 6 pm. The point is you need a great quality of life. That's just not possible the way most people choose to do this business.

When you get *really* good at this transactional model—you know all the word tracks and closes; you know how to give a great walk-around presentation; you know the business inside and out—you could increase your closing ratio to maybe 35%. That gets you to second base. You're swinging 60 times, and selling between 18 and 30 cars. And that's where most sales people get stuck. They're frustrated and angry because they can't seem to make it to the next level. They work harder and harder, and they still can't get past 2nd base. Many of them stay stuck between 8 and 16 cars—forever—and jump from dealership to dealership looking for their magic!

They're waiting for the next Up . . .

Hoping they have good credit . . .

Hoping the manager is in a good mood . . .

Hoping they like the car inventory . . .

Hoping the used car manager gives them enough for the trade . . .

And they're praying they don't spend 9 hours serving 2 customers only to wind up with a couple of mini-deals.

Most sales people live right there. To get to 100 cars on 2nd base, you have to talk to 300 people, which is 15 people a day, and that's not possible.

You just can't take that many swings at bat per day. So what do you do? You work more hours. You live at the dealership. You neglect your family, friends, and your health.

If that's where you are, I hear you. I've been there, too. And I want to give you some hope. Here's the deal: if you started reading this book looking for a silver bullet—a new word track or close that's going to magically lift your numbers—then listen closely. There are no silver bullets to fix the transactional model of selling. You can't get to 100 cars a month that way. You just can't.

The good news is there's another way. It's called the Relationship Model of selling, and with that small mindset shift—you CAN get to a higher number of cars a month, without sacrificing your family life.

Here's How to Hit a Home Run (Over and Over and Over)

There are sales people who have figured out how to get all the way to 3rd base. They're selling between 35 and 50 cars a month. How? They marry the traditional transactional model our industry teaches with the RELATIONSHIP model. With relationships, you're only talking to people who already KNOW YOU. It's not what you know, and it's not who you know. It's WHO KNOWS YOU!

When you wait on a combination of dealer-driven opportunities *and* people who already know you, your closing ratio goes up to maybe

60%. It's better than 1st or 2nd base, but it's still a trap. You're still "stuck" at 35–50 cars. I realize you may dream of someday being trapped at that level. But you can do so much better.

We have proven that there is a way to get to 100 or whatever your home run is and it's very simple. Switch your business model to 100% relationships. That means you never wait on another dealer-driven opportunity. Dealer advertising—doesn't affect you. Bad economy? People you know still need cars, and they'll be coming straight to you. When you work only with relationships—waiting on people who know you (and referrals)—you're going to close more than 80% of the people you talk to. That means if you talk to 40 people, you're going to sell 30 of them.

To get to 100? You just talk to a 120 a month, or 6 people a day, and that is doable. Six people a day is totally reasonable. This is everything that I want to teach you. How to move from the transactional model you were taught to the more natural relationship model. This book will get you started with tactical moves you can make every day. Everything we talk about here has been tried and proven. It works. All that's required of you is to make that mindset shift. It's all in the relationships, it's all about people.

Here's another way to look at it. When you started working in this business, you learned a simple strategy. You want the customer to like you, trust you, believe you and then they'd buy from you. In the transactional way of doing business, it takes time to sell the customer on liking, believing, and trusting you. But in the relationship model, you don't need to do any of that "selling" because they *already* know, like, believe and trust you. So, all they have to do is buy.

What's your magic number? Where are you stuck right now? 8 cars? 16? 25? 40? I want you to know that you can absolutely sail past wherever you are right now and hit home runs month after month, year after year and then pass your business on to your children. You just have to learn a different way of doing things.

100 cars a month.

Impossible?

Listen to me. Everything is impossible until it's done.

We've done it. And so can you.

Keep reading . . .

Here's What I Do on a Daily Basis to Sell 100 Cars a Month

Selling 100 cars a month isn't rocket science. It's about consistently taking the right actions. Don't worry, you won't have to memorize any new scripts or word tracks. You don't have to remember another 27 Steps to the Sale. You already know everything you need to know. Are you ready to learn what you need to do? Here it is:

Stop. Selling.

Car sales people have probably the worst reputations possible. Customers come in already armed with information they looked up on the internet. They already don't trust us. In fact, they often look for any excuse to hate us. You can't fight this with sales tactics. That's just going to make them dig in further.

Instead, stop trying to sell a car, and start focusing on solving problems. Serve the customer by asking questions, finding out what they need, then helping them get what they want. That's it. (See? I told you it was simple.)

Of course, if it's really that simple, why isn't everyone selling 100 cars? You got me. I have no idea. It might have something to do with how many people they talk to. Or maybe it's just that they believe they are 24 car-a-month people, so that's what they get. Whatever the reason, you have the opportunity to change it for yourself right now.

You want to make more money? Sell more cars.

You want to sell more cars? Talk to more people!

The more people you talk to, the more you will sell. It's simple.

Here's what I do to make sure I'm serving my customers at the highest level.

1. **I get myself out there as much as possible**, so I'm building new relationships all the time. This is the most important piece of the puzzle. You have to talk to people and find low-pressure ways to let them know what you do. The more people you talk to, the more people will come see you at the store. It's a numbers game. Don't rely on the company advertising to bring people to you. You have to get out there and do your own leg work. Talk to people in line at the grocery store, at your kids' soccer games, or at church. Be active in your community, and support organizations you believe in with your time and your money. Even when you're at the upper sales levels, you still need to advertise for yourself. We have a local community center where I have a banner on the wall—people see that and ask about me. You want everyone to be familiar with your name.

2. **I will do just about anything for a customer** (as long as it's legal). Serving customers goes beyond greeting them at the door and taking them on a demo ride. You want these people to be friends for life. So, help them out any way you can. Did they happen to mention they need someone to fix their roof? Do you know a good contractor? Hook them up! Does your customer own a restaurant? Take your family out to eat there. Patronize your customers' businesses. Show them you appreciate them. How else can you help? What about calling a tow truck for them, if they happen to get a flat tire? Maybe you could send them tickets to the local ball game, if you know they are fans. Get creative and help them any way you can.

3. **I treat everybody the same.** Do you have a habit of judging whether someone can afford a new car just by looking at them? The thing is you really don't know their background or anything about them until you get to know them. It's just so much easier to treat everyone the same—like royalty! It doesn't matter how they're dressed or what kind of car they drive, I treat them all the same. They all deserve my best. When you adopt this mindset, that everyone deserves to be treated like royalty, everything gets easier.

4. **I am patient with my customers.** I listen more than I speak. This is a huge key. Listen to what they want and need. Then solve their problem from there. If someone comes to you with a need, and you fill it, why wouldn't they buy from you? I know it's popular for dealerships to teach sales people how to "sell" using scripts and word tracks and pre-formulated steps to the sale. But I've never done that. It always struck me as made-up generic words trying to manipulate people. Every customer is unique, so it's impossible to use generic words to cover every situation. People can feel when you're just giving a canned answer. Just like they can tell if you're happy to talk to them.

Fortunately, I had good managers who encouraged me to figure out my own way of selling. They weren't pushing the scripts. And over time, I learned my own way of talking to people. I talk to every customer like they are my friend. I just use my regular language. I ask questions. I find out what they need. Then I solve their needs. It's so much easier that way.

5. **I stay "front of mind" with all my customers.** Every customer you meet should be a customer for life. If your neighbor comes home with a new car, and they didn't buy it from you, shame on you! Your job is to build a giant customer base and serve them

so well that they always come back. But people don't buy cars everyday. It's a purchase that they may not think about again for another 4 or 5 years. So, help them remember you. Send them an email newsletter every now and then. Call to check in and see if they are still happy with their recent purchase. Encourage them to call you, not the scheduling department, whenever they need an oil change or service. Anytime they think about something automotive related, they should think of you. I've always had the same cell phone number, and I give it out to every customer I serve. It's engraved on a special keychain I give them. They know they can call me at that number, and they do.

6. **I tell the truth—every time.** I'm not smart enough to remember what I tell everybody unless it's the truth. So, I have some simple formulas that stay the same for every customer. That way, I always know how I came to a particular number. If I don't know the answer to a question, I say so. There's nothing wrong with saying, "I don't know the answer to that, but I will find out and get back to you as fast as I can."

7. **I deliver what I promise—every time.** This is part of telling the truth. If you say you're going to call back next week, do it. If you say you're going to have the paperwork in an hour, have it ready.

Occasionally, it's not possible to deliver on a promise. When that happens, contact the customer immediately and let them know what happened and what you're going to do to remedy any issues that might arise. Don't put it off thinking they'll forget. They won't. When you own up to mistakes or things you can't deliver on, people will usually be forgiving and happy to work together toward a solution.

8. **I sell from stock.** Maybe 3 out of 100 cars I sell are dealer trades. It just takes too much time to work that way. Locating, setting up drivers, making the customer wait two or three extra days to get the car—it slows down your pace and takes the excitement out of the experience. There are times when it's necessary to do a trade, but I try to keep it to a minimum.

9. **I have fun!** This business isn't always fun. It's not fun when you're not being yourself. It's not fun when you're not successful. It's not fun when it's not easy or customers don't like you. It's frustrating and stressful when you're constantly focused on making your numbers. Yes, numbers are important. But it's equally important to be at ease with a customer and have fun—whether or not they end up buying the car. Damian says it best in his seminar: this business gets fun when you are who you are at your best, and you get to love and care for people.

The Success Threshold

It's all well and good to understand about building relationships and selling to people you know or who are referred to you. But what if you're just starting out? What if you've moved to a new town, and you don't know anyone at all? Can you still make it to 100 cars? Absolutely!

Over the years I've been in this business, I've noticed a pattern emerge with myself and other very successful sales people. We all had to start somewhere. We all had our first day on the job where we just waited for people to walk onto the lot. We all waited on Ups for a time. Our managers told us that was the job. Wait for people to show up, and sell them.

After a while, though, something happens. If you're good at taking care of your customers—and I mean really good—then they tell their friends. They send their sons and daughters in to see you. Total strangers come in to see you because someone you served in the past told them to. And one day, that customer needs a new car and they come back to see you, too. I always say if I serve a customer once, they won't have any reason to buy from someone else.

It's a subtle shift at first. You might not even notice it. A few referrals start trickling in, and you keep waiting on Ups. Then more and more people start asking specifically for you, and they start making appointments. There's less time to walk the floor, but your income increases because the sales come easier. Instead of walking in defensive and cautious, your customers are genuinely happy to see you. The already trust you. They know you're going to take care of them.

One day you wake up and realize you're not selling anymore. You're just helping people.

And you're not waiting on Ups anymore. Customers are making appointments to come see you.

It's a predictable pattern, but it doesn't always happen at the same rate. For many sales people, including me, the first three years are spent serving the Ups and building a customer base. At this point, you have to start the conversations with people. You have to initiate the relationships and let people know what you do. As time goes by, that shifts and people start coming to you asking questions about cars. They already know what you do, so they come to you with their needs.

Year 3 seems to be the tipping point. By year 4 or 5, they are still building their base, but the monthly numbers grow more rapidly. More and more repeats and referrals start coming in. Your business builds itself at this point. The better you serve people, and the more you get yourself out there, the faster your business will grow. People will stay loyal to you.

Every sales person is different. It took me 15 years to get to 100 cars a month. I didn't reach the tipping point really until year 7. Part of that was because during the economic crisis in 2008 and 2009 nobody bought a car unless they absolutely had to. But because I had a solid base of customers, I managed to survive those two years. I was still doing 25 cars, when most people were lucky to get 6 or 7. They were also closing my store, so I had no inventory to sell from. We scrambled to buy from other places just to have something to sell.

There are two other reasons it took me so long to reach that 100 milestone. First, I didn't know anyone who had sold 100. I didn't know it was something that was possible. Second, I wasn't aware of what I was doing right or wrong. I simply did what felt right to me. Later, as I got to know Damian and he coached me along, I realized what felt right was right. And all I needed to do was focus on doing more of what was working. Once I did that, I went from selling around 50 a month to selling 100 in a little over a year. It all accelerated so quickly, once I started focusing on exactly the right things.

You're lucky. You don't have those two strikes against you. Because you're reading this book, you know that 100 cars a month is totally possible. And you know what you need to do. That means your transition time can be so much shorter than mine.

Here's a Different Timeline.

Instead of thinking about how many years you might have to spend—just think about the levels you need to reach. And focus on *your* next level. If you currently sell fewer than 20 cars, that's where you want to focus. Don't think about 50 or 100. Those levels are too far away, they won't feel achievable. 20 cars. That's it. That's all you have to do. Then once you've hit 20, take a little while to enjoy that. Celebrate that achievement. Then set your sights on the next level—40 cars.

In my experience, these are the thresholds or levels you'll want to focus on:

20 cars a month—if you can sell 1, you can sell 20. That's believable. You'll get there.

40 cars a month—if you can sell 20, you can sell 40. Again, believable. You might even know people at that level in your store.

50 cars a month—if you can sell 40, you can sell 50. It's only 10 more. You can do it.

Do you see how this works? It's just small boosts up the ladder. If you can sell 50 cars a month, you can do just about anything—including reaching the 100+ level. So, challenge yourself. At 50, you can do 60. At 60, you can do 80. At 80, well 100 is just around the corner.

A few years ago, I bought a house on a lake. And I figured I'd wait a year before I bought a boat. But once I moved in, *everybody* had a boat. So, I got a used one for a little while and it was okay. But it didn't take long to realize I had the ugliest boat on the lake! The next year, I went to the local marina to get a really nice one for myself. I didn't know anything about boats other than that they float in water. So, the sales person took me out and showed me all the super-cool things this boat could do. He revved the engine and spun around creating huge, crazy wakes. And all I kept thinking was *yeah, I'm not doing THAT!*

Eventually, I said, "Look, I'm a total beginner at this. Two weeks ago, I didn't even know what an outboard was. Just show me what NOT to do." And things got simpler from there. I knew I could figure out all the cool things I *could* do later on.

I use that logic a lot when I'm teaching people to sell cars. Everyone has their own personal style, and their own ways of selling. All I want to teach you is what not to do. Once you get the behaviors and mindsets right, everything else just falls into place.

So, Here's My List of What NOT To Do As You're Climbing To That Next Level.

0 to 20 cars—

Don't use social media for personal use. It's a complete distraction. Turn off your notifications, and don't log on until you're home and relaxing. And limit your business use of social media to the few activities that actually do help you sell cars. Facebook and Instagram and all the rest take your mind off the game. You don't see professional baseball players reading Twitter while they're in the outfield. They keep their mind in the present moment, and focus on the job they are there to do. Leave your personal life out of your business. Practice being present and respectful to everyone.

Don't let the customer take a demo ride by themselves. You are there to provide an experience for the customer. If that boat salesman had just sent me off on my own, I don't think I could have even pulled away from the dock. Help them. Show them how things work. Make sure they are comfortable inside the car. This might be the first new model they've ever ridden in. Some of the computers and touch screens can be intimidating, especially for people unfamiliar with technology. Just because you understand it doesn't mean they do. Create a comfortable, enjoyable experience.

21 to 40—

Don't be too busy to answer the phone. You must be available for people to talk to you. Potential customers are going to call you and email you and come into the store to see you. YOU, not someone else. And they aren't going to wait until it's convenient for you. Taking care of your relationships—that's your job. When my customers come into the dealership and I'm not there—they won't even talk to a manager. They just say they'll come back another time. They don't want to deal with anyone else. They want to talk to me. And I work hard to make it that way.

I hand every customer of mine a keychain with my cell phone number on it. And I tell them to call me anytime if they need something. Do people call me in the middle of the night? Sometimes. But think about it. If someone is calling their car salesman in the middle of the night, they probably really need help. And I am happy to be the person who gets them out of a tough spot. Why? Well, first because I genuinely care that they're stuck, and I'm going to help them if I can. But also because they are going to tell everyone they know how they got a flat tire 100 miles away from home. And they're going to tell people I am the one who helped them. To make it easy on myself, I have a towing company that I use all the time. When a customer calls me from the side of the road, I just make a quick call and it's all taken care of.

Don't be forgotten. At this stage, you are still building your customer base. So, it's up to you to keep in contact with people. It's critical that you train your customers to think about you and call you for everything related to their transportation needs. Send an email newsletter once a month, at a minimum. My newsletter usually has a few CSI surveys with nice comments from my customers. We might put in a joke of the day or a recipe, and the rest is just deals we have going on at the moment.

We have a newsletter template available for you here: AutoTrainingAcademy.com/newsletter-template

Also, encourage your customers to call *you* to schedule oil changes or service. Yes, it takes a little extra effort to schedule them with the service department, but it's worth it. They will come to rely on you to take care of them whenever they need something for their car. I want to be the one taking care of them for life. I want them to call me as much as possible.

I've had customers go and buy a different brand vehicle from someone else, and they come back to me with horror stories about their experience. They tell me they are never leaving me again. That's what I want to hear. I work hard to earn that kind of loyalty from every customer.

40 to 50—

Don't try to do it alone. At this stage, it's time to get an assistant. I waited way too long before admitting I needed help, and it cost me time. The best use of your time is serving customers. The longer you're in business, the more customers you'll have to serve each day. So, it's important to pay close attention to where you're spending your valuable hours. Your assistant can do things like answer the phone, schedule service appointments, take care of your social media, even write and send out your newsletter. You don't have to start by paying for a full-time person. Damian hired an assistant for 2 hours a day at first (and he did it when he was only selling 15 cars).

I think the most important job for an assistant is to answer the phone. I want to train people to call me for everything, but I can't always be there to answer them immediately. So, having a live person on the other end of the phone is so critical to build that trust in the customer's mind. An assistant can answer quick questions, and she can help diffuse any upset customers or bring problems to my attention, if necessary. Once I got an assistant, I went from 50 to 70 really quickly.

Don't doubt. There's a thing that happens when people reach 40 cars a month. They believe in themselves. They know they can go to any dealership they want and replicate their success. When you feel that happening to you, when your confidence starts to soar, notice it and pay attention. You'll probably still have little voices whispering doubts into your head, but you don't have to listen to them. You've proven you can sell at this level. You have the recipe, and you can go as far as you want to. Go do it!

50 to 100+ –

Don't wait on Ups. Ever. At this level, you aren't going to have time for anyone but your own customers and the referrals they send. Still, it will be tempting to take care of someone who just wanders into the store and looks lost. You can still serve them and stay on course by greeting them and kindly introducing them to another sales person. Even if they have cash in hand, and are ready to buy that car outside right now—walk them over to someone else. You've spent a lot of time and effort to build your own customer base. They are the only ones who should be getting your time and attention.

Don't let numbers hold you back. At this point, why limit yourself to a measly 100 cars a month? The first time I hit 100, I actually sold 101. And I didn't even know it for a couple of days because we were so busy helping people. By now, you understand that the only limit to how much business you can do is inside your own head. My best month so far has been 144 cars. Really. But other months, I might do 85. It all evens out in the long run. And you know what? I don't even think about the numbers anymore. I don't have time. Rather than thinking *there goes car number 83 for the month*, just focus on the next customer. How can you help them? What do they need? Think about the customers and the numbers will take care of themselves.

How long it takes to get to the next threshold is up to you. Just realize that even though it takes time, you will get there. Be patient with yourself, and you'll be amazed at how far you can go.

You Are the Only Thing Standing In Your Way

Now that you know what's possible, it's natural for your brain to come up with all sorts of reasons why it's not possible for you. Objections, reasons, excuses—whatever you want to call them—they're not real. They are made up in your head. And you get to decide whether you're going to believe them or not.

Make no mistake, your brain is very smart. It knows exactly what to say to keep you stuck where you are. Those reasons it comes up with will make total sense to you—until they don't. Here's what I know from experience. Everything you need is already inside of you. There's no secret handshake. There's no magic word track. There's nothing else you need. Just belief in yourself, and some time to make it happen.

If I can do this, anyone can do this. *You* can do this.

Got it?

Good!

That's not going to stop the excuses from showing up, though. So, let's go over the most common ones right now. I want you to see that even though they sound like legitimate reasons why you can't get to your next level, in fact, they're just excuses. Smoke and mirrors.

"I'm not smart enough." It's not about smarts. It's about loving what you do. If you love helping people, you can succeed. This business is all about numbers, but not the numbers your GM probably tells you to focus on. It's all about the number of people you talk to. The more people you meet and serve, the more cars you will sell. That's just basic math. You don't need a college education to understand this business. You just have to care.

"I'm already working 7 days a week, and I never see my family as it is." The key is *not* working 7 days a week. You want to work less and provide a better future for your family. I know the car business doesn't understand this. Their paradigm is that everybody works 6 or 7 days a week. That's just how they teach people to sell cars. But it doesn't have to be that way. In fact, it *shouldn't* be that way. You're not a slave. You have to find a way to do business so that your life has meaning. And your life has no meaning if all you are is the next sale.

There's more to life than being a sales person. Following Damian's plan and building those relationships is how I did it. It takes time, obviously. It doesn't happen overnight. But it does work, and it allows you to have fun at your job and plenty of free time for your family. I know it can be difficult to believe that working less will be better in the long run. But I know the end result is worth it. You owe it to yourself to try it.

Damian likes to say working 6 days a week and selling 10 cars a month isn't right. If you're stuck in that situation, the business isn't working for you. You're not in the wrong business, you're in your business wrong. This business is all about people. If you're looking at your paycheck rather than how many people you can help today—you're going about it backwards. If you can intentionally put yourself in front of as many people as possible, without it being all about you, the end of the month is going to be profitable. You're worried about the end of the month and 10 cars. I'm worried about getting in front of people *today*, and shaking someone's hand—getting to know them and their needs. Focus on what you're doing one day at a time, and the end of the month will take care of itself. I promise.

"I have a hard time using the sales tactics my managers are giving me." You have to be who you are. I was never comfortable having a canned generic answer for everything any customer said. So, I didn't use the word tracks and scripts they gave me. I was just myself. I asked questions from a place of genuine curiosity and caring, then I did my best to help the customer. Sometimes managers will tell you that you're being too nice, and you'll never succeed if you're too nice. I hate that. That's how our business got such a bad reputation to begin with. If you just be yourself, be nice, and help—you're going to stand out, and you're going to see your business grow. Just help people out, whatever way you do that is fine.

"It's great for other people, but I'm barely selling 10 / 20 / _____ cars now. How can I possibly sell 100?" How do you know unless you try? If you like helping people, it has nothing to do with the cars. Even if you sell something completely different—appliances or real estate—focus on the people. I didn't know anything about car sales when I first started. I was working in a warehouse and making about $50,000 a year. I knew I wouldn't be making any more than that in 3 or 5 years. I needed a change. So a friend of mine told me about selling cars. I just decided to give it a try. I didn't know anything about numbers. I didn't even know how much money the sales person made off a car. I just felt like it was an opportunity, and I owed it to myself to try it. I'm not some specially-gifted sales guru or anything. I'm just a guy helping a lot of people. You might try and fail, but it's the trying that counts.

"What happens if I go backward from month to month?" I don't look at it like that. The end of the month isn't the most important thing, serving the customer is the most important thing. Do I always hit 100? No. Sometimes I sell 140, sometimes it's 75 or 80. That's still pretty good. It all averages out over the year. I can't stress enough how important it is to take your mind off the numbers and just talk to more people.

Those are the most common objections I hear from sales people, but I'm sure there are more. Your brain will undoubtedly come up with some really creative "reasons" why you can't make it to the next level.

Don't listen. Believe in yourself.

And get a mentor, coach, or someone who will inspire you to keep moving forward. Find a person who will hold you accountable to your goals and help you see what you're doing right. You don't have to do it alone.

So, What Are You Gonna Do Now?

This book isn't for everybody. Selling 100 cars a month might not be for you. That's okay. The strategies and tactics I've mentioned in this book and the ones Damian teaches still work no matter what level you're at. So, go back through and notice the pieces that speak to you. You don't have to use every idea in this book, but I challenge you to find at least 3 that you can take to work with you tomorrow and implement right away. Over time as you reach 20, 40, 50—you might find out that 100 cars a month really IS for you after all.

Your mindset should be all about the next 4-minute mile. I would never in a million years have thought that I could do 100. I believed I might do 60, even though that was a huge number. Once I got there, I knew I could get to 70. Every milestone you reach, you smash that 4-minute mile barrier and there's a new bar to reach.

Grow at your own pace. Be yourself. And have fun.

That's what it's all about.

Now, think about what you've learned throughout this book and answer those questions again for me. It's my hope that your answers have changed a little.

Why do customers buy from you?

Where are you now with your sales?

What's your dream? How many cars would you be happy selling?

You can't go back to the way things were. You've read my story, so you can't pretend that 100 cars a month isn't possible. Which means you have two choices—you can settle for where you are now and decide that's good enough for you. OR you can decide you're going to reach that next milestone. Decide that you're going to figure it out. Whatever it takes.

You're going to get what you deserve—financial freedom and work satisfaction. It's your time.

If that's what you want, Damian and I are here to help you. And you're invited to join a group of people just like you—people determined to reach their goals no matter what. People who support each other and have your back when you're not sure what to do next. If you're interested in joining us, keep reading . . .

You're Invited To Join Us

I had an advantage that most people don't have. I had a mentor on my side. I had Damian who kept believing in me and lifting me up to that next level. If you would like that same advantage, you're invited to check out our advanced training programs at the Auto Training Academy.

The 100 Car Club is a group of high achievers striving for their next level. Ali Reda and other guest trainers personally mentor you, help you blast through the obstacles in your way, and celebrate your wins every month. Want to get to 100 cars a month? This is the fastest way to do it!

Find out more and join us here:

www. AutoTrainingAcademy.com/100-club

Appendix

A Note From Damian:

Below are just a tiny handful of the reviews, testimonials, and thank-you notes Ali has received from his customers over the past few years. I am adding them here because I want you to read them and pay attention to the themes that are repeated over and over again.

Listen to Ali's customers talk about how he treats them like family, and how often they refer others to him. Strive for comments like these from your customers! THIS is how you sell 100 cars—relationships.

Melanie S.
Westland, MI
⬇ **0** friends
📷 1 review

   9/18/2014

I was very pleased with my transaction. **Ali Reda** was
recommended by a family member who has used him for
her leasing needs for the last 10 yrs. I was impressed -
went seamless and I am very happy. I have already
recommended Ali to a co-worker and will contact him in 24
months for my next lease.

Was this review ...?

 Useful   Funny   Cool

Moe H.
Dearborn, MI
⬇ **42** friends
📷 **3** reviews

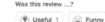 6/13/2016

The experience was perfect. **Ali Reda** was professional
and streamlined the process smoothly.

Was this review ...?

 Useful 1   Funny   Cool

Rabeah B.
Dearborn, MI
⬇ **0** friends
📷 1 review

   9/8/2016

Ali Reda has been the most well organized, pleasant
salesman I have ever dealt with. He is really on top of his
work and works extremely professionally. This has been
my third purchase from Ali and I would recommend him to
anyone. He is the best salesman I have ever worked with
and his service is second to none. Thank you for the great
experience once again!

Was this review ...?

Useful 1   Funny   Cool

Daryl Wizinsky with Ali M Reda at ♥ Les Stanford Chevrolet Cadillac.
October 3 · Dearborn, MI · 🌐

Thank you Ali M Reda for the amazing experience. Mostly just keeping it real. I am grateful and thankful for my new car!!! I have never had a car this nice. I am really grateful. Thank you to everyone who has helped me get here and to god!!!

To be honest, Ali M Reda is one of the most standup guys I have ever met.. I was blown away!!! I am a customer for life!!!! His character is what this world should be built on!!!

 **Douglas Laura** Awesome ride
Like · Reply · ⭕ 1 · October 3 at 4:24pm

 Les Stanford Chevrolet Cadillac Congratulations on your new Escalade Daryl Wizinsky! It's a beautiful vehicle and we're sure that you will enjoy it. Be safe and happy!
Like · Reply · October 3 at 4:25pm

 Daryl Wizinsky Lots and Lots of referrals to come to Ali M Reda This was truly an amazing experience.. Hats off to you guys for taking care of an ex F & I Manager and keeping it real.
Like · Reply · October 3 at 4:28pm

 Robert Khoury You're welcome brother! 🙂 Didn't I tell you there is no other like Ali Reda! 🙂
Like · Reply · ⭕ 1 · October 3 at 5:03pm

 Daryl Wizinsky He kept it real.. Ali M Reda and I have a lot of respect for each other.. And at the end of the day, this transaction further made my point about making sure we service our clients the right way.. Not our opinions, thoughts, wants or making it about collecting a pay check!!!
Like · Reply · October 3 at 5:06pm

Ali T. Charara ▶ **Ali M Reda**
September 25, 2014 · Dearborn Heights, MI · 👥

I am writing to compliment Ali M Reda for the great service and
professionalism that went far beyond the ordinary. Thank you for your
outstanding service, you have earned a repeat customer and a referral to
anyone who asks where I bought the truck.
You are a first class

👍 33

Ali Saad One of the best out there!
September 25, 2014 at 9:30am · 👍 2

Ali Mozham Reda the best
September 25, 2014 at 1:11pm · 👍 1

Maureen Wright ▶ **Ali M Reda**
May 6 · 👥

Ali M Reda, we could not have asked for a smoother transaction today. Thank
You so much for all of your assistance. You are a true professional. — 😊
feeling thankful.

👍 1

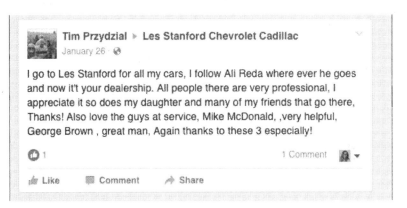

Tim Przydzial ▸ **Les Stanford Chevrolet Cadillac**
January 26 · 🌐

I go to Les Stanford for all my cars, I follow Ali Reda where ever he goes and now it't your dealership. All people there are very professional, I appreciate it so does my daughter and many of my friends that go there, Thanks! Also love the guys at service, Mike McDonald, ,very helpful, George Brown , great man, Again thanks to these 3 especially!

👍 1   1 Comment

👍 Like   💬 Comment   ↗ Share

Alexander Beydoun ▸ **Ali M Reda**
June 4, 2015 · 👥

Thank you for making sure my parents are taken care of.
Kindest regards from Dallas, Texas

Mohamad Abdallah ▸ **Ali M Reda**
April 3, 2015 · 👥

No one gives you excellent customer service like Ali...our family and friends lease and buy from him only!! You Da Man Ali!!! 2016 🏎 Camaro next year Al!

"ALI REDA is a great asset to Les Standford. He gave me..." - drali3

ALI REDA is a great asset to Les Standford. He gave me EXCEPTIONAL SERVICE and within two days closed on my new cadillac for my wife. Ali had the paperwork ready, keys ready, and all I had to do was sign and I was off. He was very friendly and I HIGHLY recommend him! Thanks ALI.
READ LESS

CUSTOMER SERVICE	★★★★★
QUALITY OF WORK	★★★★★
FRIENDLINESS	★★★★★
PRICING	★★★★★
OVERALL EXPERIENCE	★★★★★
RECOMMEND DEALER	**YES**

March 30, 2011

★★★★★
DEALERSHIP RATING

"Customer Service at Les Stanford was excellent. Ali Reda..." - Happy:)

Customer Service at Les Stanford was excellent. Ali Reda surpassed "great" customer service. He worked with my husband and I until we were found he perfect vehicle that met our needs and our spending limit. He helped us decide on our Lease vs. Buy option and made sure we knew exactly where our money was going. He was exremely friendly and went above and beyond by staying in close contact with us. We never felt pressured to get into an agreement. Everyone at this dealership was friendly and approachable. I am so happy we went through Ali Reda and the Les Stanford family for our purchase. I highly recommend them.

READ LESS

CUSTOMER SERVICE	★★★★★
QUALITY OF WORK	★★★★★
FRIENDLINESS	★★★★★
PRICING	★★★★★
OVERALL EXPERIENCE	★★★★★
RECOMMEND DEALER	**YES**

March 09, 2011

★★★★★
DEALERSHIP RATING

"Ali is an excellent salesman! He leads you to the car you..." - Bob2953

Ali is an excellent salesman! He leads you to the car you need and want. This is the second vehicle that I have bought from him and he finds you the best price he can. I consider Ali a good friend or more preciously, he make me feel like it!

Thank you for another great experience!

READ LESS

CUSTOMER SERVICE	★★★★★
QUALITY OF WORK	★★★★★
FRIENDLINESS	★★★★★
PRICING	★★★★★
OVERALL EXPERIENCE	★★★★★
RECOMMEND DEALER	**YES**

January 19, 2011

★★★★★
DEALERSHIP RATING

"Overall best experience purchasing a vehicle, I would..." - **hdaghe2003**

Overall best experience purchasing a vehicle, I would recommend Ali Reda to anyone, he made the purchase incredibly smooth, easy and effortless, especially since time was a factor for me he made it all happen. All my previous bad experiences purchasing a car went out the window while working with Ali and dealership manager Mike Lowe who checked in with me to make sure I was happy and satisfied, great guys, friendly and to the point. If anyone wants to buy or lease a Grn car or even a Cadillac ALI REDA is the go to guy.

Thank You And Much Appreciated

H. Dagher
READ LESS

CUSTOMER SERVICE	★★★★★
QUALITY OF WORK	★★★★★
FRIENDLINESS	★★★★★
PRICING	★★★★★
OVERALL EXPERIENCE	★★★★★
RECOMMEND DEALER	**YES**

December 27, 2011

★★★★★
DEALERSHIP RATING

"This was my best experience with a car salesman. Ali Reda..." - loubnamfayz

This was my best experience with a car salesman. Ali Reda is honest, friendly, cares about his customers, works hard with a great attitude to help provide what his customers are looking for in a vehicle.

Thank you Ali

Loubna M Fayz
READ LESS

CUSTOMER SERVICE	★★★★★
QUALITY OF WORK	★★★★★
FRIENDLINESS	★★★★★
PRICING	★★★★★
OVERALL EXPERIENCE	★★★★★
RECOMMEND DEALER	YES

December 26, 2011

★★★★★
DEALERSHIP RATING

"This 2012 Malibu is the 2nd car I have purchased from Ali..." - seanie143

This 2012 Malibu is the 2nd car I have purchased from Ali Reda. After Bill Wink Chevrolet closed I didn't know where to go. I found out that Ali was at Les Stanford so I followed him here. It was the BEST decision I have made! Ali has helped my mother, brother, and me to find the right car. He knows what I want and how to get me the best deal possible. I recommend him to everyone I know. He truly is the BEST car salesman! I am COMPLETELY SATISFIED with him and know that he has taken GREAT care of me!
READ LESS

CUSTOMER SERVICE	★★★★★
QUALITY OF WORK	★★★★★
FRIENDLINESS	★★★★★
PRICING	★★★★★
OVERALL EXPERIENCE	★★★★★
RECOMMEND DEALER	YES

September 25, 2012

★ ★ ★ ★ ★
DEALERSHIP RATING

"I had a very pleasant experience dealing with Mr. Reda...." - gdaholui

I had a very pleasant experience dealing with Mr. Reda. He was very courtious, thorough, and extremely helpful.

I believe Mr. Reda's experience and knowledge made our purchase very smooth and pleasant.
READ LESS

CUSTOMER SERVICE	★ ★ ★ ★ ★
QUALITY OF WORK	★ ★ ★ ★ ★
FRIENDLINESS	★ ★ ★ ★ ★
PRICING	★ ★ ★ ★ ★
OVERALL EXPERIENCE	★ ★ ★ ★ ★
RECOMMEND DEALER	**YES**

January 21, 2014

★ ★ ★ ★ ★
DEALERSHIP RATING

"Best treatment. Courteous and If it was a different..." - fridha

Best treatment. Courteous and If it was a different person I would not have got the vehicle. I like his attitude and I will my recomend him for my family and friends.
READ LESS

CUSTOMER SERVICE	★ ★ ★ ★ ★
QUALITY OF WORK	★ ★ ★ ★ ★
FRIENDLINESS	★ ★ ★ ★ ★
PRICING	★ ★ ★ ★ ★
OVERALL EXPERIENCE	★ ★ ★ ★ ★
RECOMMEND DEALER	**YES**

July 28, 2014

★ ★ ★ ★ ★
DEALERSHIP RATING

"Allways satisfied with Ali Reda and Les Stanford " - maya1226

This's my 4th vehicle from Les Stanford and my 9th car from Ali Reda. I fallowed Ali from Bill Wink Chevrolet and for good reason. He exceeds all expectations as a salesman, and would highly recommend him to anyone in search of a Chevy.

READ LESS

CUSTOMER SERVICE	★ ★ ★ ★ ★
QUALITY OF WORK	★ ★ ★ ★ ★
FRIENDLINESS	★ ★ ★ ★ ★
PRICING	★ ★ ★ ★ ★
OVERALL EXPERIENCE	★ ★ ★ ★ ★
RECOMMEND DEALER	**YES**

May 11, 2013

★★★★★
DEALERSHIP RATING

"i jihad chamas have been dealing with Ali Reda and Les..." - jkchamas

i jihad chamas have been dealing with Ali Reda and Les Stanford for a long time. i have been treated like family very friendly and trustworthy. the best salesman i have ever dealt with and the the dealership as a whole is top notch
READ LESS

CUSTOMER SERVICE	★★★★★
QUALITY OF WORK	★★★★★
FRIENDLINESS	★★★★★
PRICING	★★★★☆
OVERALL EXPERIENCE	★★★★★
RECOMMEND DEALER	**YES**

November 05, 2013

★★★★★
DEALERSHIP RATING

"Les Stanford is my favorite Chevrolet dealer. I always..." - carly313

Les Stanford is my favorite Chevrolet dealer. I always get my cars from Ali Reda. Fast and friendly service. recommended dealership to all my family and friends.

READ LESS

CUSTOMER SERVICE	★★★★★
QUALITY OF WORK	★★★★★
FRIENDLINESS	★★★★★
PRICING	★★★★★
OVERALL EXPERIENCE	★★★★★
RECOMMEND DEALER	**YES**

May 02, 2012

★★★★★
DEALERSHIP RATING

"I recently purchased a new Cadillac from Ali Reda at Les..." - Dr. Ron

I recently purchased a new Cadillac from Ali Reda at Les Stanford and I am extremely satisfied. Ali went above and beyond to get me the vehicle I wanted at a great price. He made sure I was able to take advantage of several rebates that I was unaware of prior to inquiring about a new car. Ali made sure to make the whole transaction hassle free, finalized all the details, and all I had to do was walk in and sign and pick up my new, gleaming Cadillac. I have already referred several friends in the market for new vehicles and I have no doubt they will be well taken care of with Ali. I usually don't even care to take the time to write reviews, but I was so impressed with Ali's service that I felt compelled to spread the word. Les Stanford is a beautiful dealership with the best selection around, that coupled with the fact that they have the best salesperson around makes going there an easy choice.
READ LESS

CUSTOMER SERVICE	★★★★★
QUALITY OF WORK	★★★★★
FRIENDLINESS	★★★★★
PRICING	★★★★★
OVERALL EXPERIENCE	★★★★★
RECOMMEND DEALER	**YES**

March 04, 2016

★★★★★
DEALERSHIP RATING

★★★★★
EMPLOYEE RATING

"Second lease with Ali" - Okange22

This is my second lease with Ali Reda, as always he goes above and beyond to providing the best service possible. Puts his clients first, responds in a timely manner. If Ali can't get you something he will always have positive non aggressive sales suggestions. If it makes sense he will tell you and if it doesn't he's not hesitant to tell you the truth. Thank you Ali, as always keep up the great work.

READ LESS

CUSTOMER SERVICE	★★★★★
QUALITY OF WORK	★★★★★
FRIENDLINESS	★★★★★
PRICING	★★★★★
OVERALL EXPERIENCE	★★★★★
RECOMMEND DEALER	YES

March 15, 2016

★★★★★
DEALERSHIP RATING

★★★★★
EMPLOYEE RATING

"Best service and prices anywhere." - rami7188

Ali Reda was by far the best car salesman ive ever dealt with. To sum it up terrific service, great prices, and exceeded my expectations. Will be back

READ LESS

CUSTOMER SERVICE	★★★★★
QUALITY OF WORK	★★★★★
FRIENDLINESS	★★★★★
PRICING	★★★★★
OVERALL EXPERIENCE	★★★★★
RECOMMEND DEALER	YES

March 17, 2016

★★★★★
DEALERSHIP RATING

★★★★★
EMPLOYEE RATING

"3rd lease with ali" - melroumi

received excellent services and i recommend him to everyone, good dealer, good salesmen. I will keep leasing from him every car i want in the future.
READ LESS

CUSTOMER SERVICE	★★★★★
QUALITY OF WORK	★★★★★
FRIENDLINESS	★★★★★
PRICING	★★★★★
OVERALL EXPERIENCE	★★★★★
RECOMMEND DEALER	**YES**

October 06, 2016

★★★★★
DEALERSHIP RATING

★★★★★
EMPLOYEE RATING

"Best Experience with Mr. Ali Reda" - Rossi

It was Perfect from all directions, and Mr. Ali Reda is the best. He is an extraordinary person with the customer from all directions. Thank you Mr. Ali , and thank you Les Stanford for having a gentleman Like Mr. Reda. I will definitely recommend Mr. Reda to my friends and family. Thanks
READ LESS

CUSTOMER SERVICE	★★★★★
QUALITY OF WORK	★★★★★
FRIENDLINESS	★★★★★
PRICING	★★★★★
OVERALL EXPERIENCE	★★★★★
RECOMMEND DEALER	**YES**

About Ali Reda

People will drive 40 minutes and pass 100 dealerships to come to me because I provide a fun atmosphere.

Ali Reda is a sales consultant at Les Stanford Chevrolet Cadillac in Dearborn, Michigan. He currently sells an average of 115 cars a month through the Relationship Model of selling.

In an effort to help other sales people reach their highest aspirations, Reda is also a faculty member at the Auto Training Academy, an online resource for sales people in the automotive business.

About Damian Boudreaux

The business of our business is people. And the key to massive success is being who you are at your best, and then figuring out how to take care of others.Master this, and you will be profitable and proud of your way of life.

Damian Boudreaux is a speaker and teacher for the automotive industry and founder of the Auto Training Academy, an online training resource for automotive sales people. His 30 years of experience selling, training, consulting, and connecting with auto professionals across the United States, South America, and Canada is the perfect recipe for those who are hungry to improve every area of their lives. He educates and inspires folks to succeed by believing in themselves, the deal, their product, their company and their service—one lifelong relationship at a time.

Boudreaux's unique approach to relationship selling has helped thousands of salespeople, service advisors, managers, and dealers double their dollars in this business—including selling 100 cars a month and beyond.